Happy Easter   1973
To Cheryl
from Norma

Kathleen Partridge's

LIGHT AT EVENTIDE

Jarrold Colour Publications

'*Hold fast to that which is good*'
DEDICATED WITH LOVE

TO MY AUNT MABEL
Whose life is uncluttered
As a new day
And wholesome
As a crusty loaf
And who believes that all religions
Should begin with tolerance and respect
For all other religions.

Sunrise, Loch Earn, Perthshire

Winter sees the mountains of the Lake District take on their mantle of snow. Fewer people venture onto the fells at this time of year but those that do may enjoy scenes of icy splendour. *Above:* Coniston. *Opposite:* Derwentwater.

LIFE IS A PRAYER

What better prayer, what better thanks
  Awakening to say
Breathing in the morning air
  'It is a lovely day'.

What better christianity
  Than kindness on the spot
Whether you have spared the time
  For kneeling down or not.

What better true religion
  Than to lift the ones who fall
To love your fellow men
  And have a heart that beats for all.

Show me the merry moments
In an ordinary sight
Like daffodils still dancing
When the storm is at its height.

The music of the hours
Not the worries and the fears
To count more joy than sorrow
In the passing of the years.

The southern counties of England have a wealth of picturesque
cottages, often situated in delightful villages. The one above
is at Chiddingfold, Surrey; that opposite at Cuckfield, Sussex.

'*He led them forth in the right way*'
THE ROAD HOME

Thankful we are, to tread the way so far.
Along the road of happiness and tears.
Seeing again, the seasons bloom and wane
Gaining a greater courage with the years.

Glad to be born, to greet the dusk and dawn
And gather loyal friends along the way.
Thankful to be, so safe, so near to Thee
Put forth a hand to bless our home this day.

In Glen Shee, Perthshire

It would be hard to imagine the English countryside without its population of birds. In the Spring, of course, they are busy building their nests and rearing the young, and clever photographers may catch them in these activities. *Above:* the Beared Tit is a colourful denizen of marshes in the east of England. *Opposite:* the Spotted Flycatcher, a regular visitor.

PRAYER FOR IMPROVEMENT

I have spoken with the voice Thou gavest
Tried to learn the wisdom Thou hast taught.
Used the little talents of my birthright
And with the courage given I have fought.

I have seen beauty in the silent places
And caught a glimpse of Heaven from a leaf
Loved the little creatures tame or timid
And found a joy of life beyond belief.

If there is something more I might accomplish
And something better that I could have done
Give me the chance to try with greater wisdom
And to complete the life I have begun.

BUSY HANDS

For busy hands that make the work a pleasure
We thank Thee every moment of the day.
For joy in duty bringing peace with leisure
We praise Thee, for there lies the happy way.

For health to take the measure of the moment
And strength to work along the given track
For faith that follows in the path of duty
And trust in God that knows no turning back.

God bless these daily labours with fulfilment
And grant the strength for our allotted span
That we may serve in spite of age or ailment
A good day's work portrays a happy man.

The moors and mountains of the North Country are sparsely populated except by sheep. They are moved down from the fells before the winter sets in to sheltered valleys. *Opposite:* Kentmere Valley, Westmorland. *Above:* Loweswater.

'None of us liveth to himself'
THE HOMELY PRAYER

Praise to Thee for all the joys of living
For all the comforts that a home contains
Make me content with what the day is giving
Bearing the losses, sharing out the gains.
Praise to Thee for sound and sight made clearer
For rain and wind, for scent and song and dew
May every evening bring Thy presence nearer
And every morning lift my heart anew.

Old houses at Canterbury, Kent

THE CROSS TO BEAR

Hard the way and high the hill
That we must climb to do Thy will.
Stony the path and rough the road
And heavy is the living load.

But many men have gone before
And all the saints have suffered more.
How dare we falter, faint, or fall
With Thou beside to carry all.

Or sink with suffering and loss
When ours is such a little cross.
We ask not for a lighter load
But just Thy Presence on the road.

The sight of farm horses working has become very rare in recent years, only a few farmers retaining them to mow or plough for a love of horses or just plain nostalgia for a past age. Fortunately Suffolks and Shires are still bred for showing.

Both these villages are tucked away off the beaten track·
Both could fairly be described as unspoilt, with cottages
of great individuality grouped around fine churches. *Above:*
East Hendred, Berkshire. *Opposite:* Heydon, Norfolk.

Prayers are often thoughts when I am working
Without a good beginning or an end.
Fragments of the plans of daily living
Telling all about it to a Friend.

Little scraps of hope and thanks and wishes
Sharing praise and problems great and small
Not the perfect prayers I should be praying
Just talking to my Maker that is all.

Such trifles are my prayers of life and people
So many tangled threads of odds and ends
Lord, gather them together in Thy goodness
And frame them in a tapestry that blends.

'*He shall direct my path*'
THE TRAVELLERS' PRAYER

St Christopher on land and sea
Use your strength to strengthen me
While journeying where life has led
Treading the path that lies ahead.

You, who make the way seem shorter
Who carried Christ across the water
St Christopher to you I pray
Guide my wanderings today.

The old mill at Hambleden, Buckinghamshire

Give me a good companion Lord
To share the hours of living
Somebody to laugh with me
Both loving and forgiving.

A friend who can accept my faults
And count my virtues dear.
Loyal to the end of life
What foe then need I fear?

These two breeds of dog summarise the two main functions of the animal with man. The corgi is today primarily a housedog and pet though once it helped herd sheep.

The countryside that surrounds the vast industrial complexes of Britain is often quite beautiful. Thus (*above*) the falls on the River Cynafon, Breconshire, are within easy reach of Cardiff, and Witton-le-Weir (*opposite*) is in Co. Durham.

'O Lord I am oppressed, undertake for me'
BECAUSE I AM OLD

Lord it is so easy to be fretful
Frail the frame in which the heart beats still
So hard it is to keep the spirit soaring
When there are lonely hours of fear to fill.

Lord give me patience for my slowing actions
Lord give me sweetness to the loving few
Lord give me kindness to the quick and active
And gratitude for all the things they do.

Lord it is so easy losing courage
To make complaint upon an ageing tongue
So fill my heart with wisdom, not resentment
And bring me understanding for the young.

'Labour not to be rich'

THIS BEAUTIFUL WORLD

For light and sunshine, dew and rain
I thank the Good Lord once again
Because I know, the flowers will grow
And all the singing grass remain.

For dusk and sunset, dawn and light
With birds that sing from morn 'til night
For flowering trees and sunny seas.
I thank Thee with my heart's delight.

Azaleas by the Woodland Pond, Richmond Park, Surrey

Time and again His love has upheld me
Lifted and carried me through.
Time and again when I floundered and faltered
He taught me to reason anew.

This I do know that God's love is abiding
In just the same way as the past
On this very day and on all my tomorrows
Life's troubles are not born to last.

Above: the county of Devon is not all seaside; it has
Dartmoor and Burrator Lake. *Opposite:* a summer's day
could be spent on the river at Knaresborough, Yorkshire.

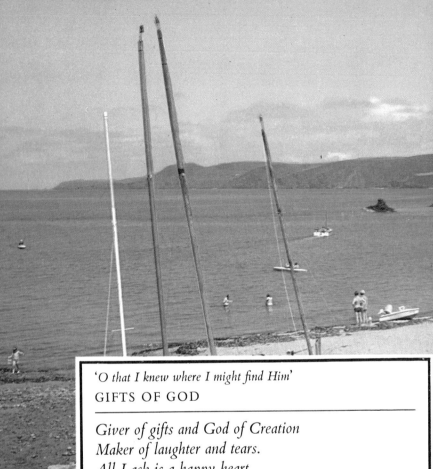

'O that I knew where I might find Him'
GIFTS OF GOD

Giver of gifts and God of Creation
Maker of laughter and tears.
All I ask is a happy heart
To carry me over the years.

A lively mind and a sense of fun
Wherever the future wends.
The courage to live and the grace to pray
And the love of a few good friends.

The beach, Aberporth, Cardiganshire, Wales

FOUND IN A FLOWER

Let there be a fragrant flower
To greet me in the garden
To prove Thy loving care
When I am praying for a pardon.

A perfect petal shining bright
Without the world's alloy
And at the dusk serenity
And in the morning . . . joy.

These pages show flowers that have grown in the cottage
gardens of England for generations, the rose and clematis.

Guard our sons, and the sons of our sons
And the generations to be
Who test their manhood and find their peace
And put their trust in the sea.

Who live by the rod, the line or a net
Or sail on the ocean free
Guard our men and the sons of our men
In the boats that put out to sea.

Above: the coastal scenery of Cornwall is of great beauty, though the jagged rocks may be a threat to shipping. This is Lizard Head. *Opposite:* cliffs on Alderney, Channel Isles.

'Suffer the little children to come unto me'
A PRAYER FOR HAPPINESS

Lord let me laugh and take my joy in living
That dreary days may bring a sense of fun
To fight resentment with some extra giving
While seeing that Thy wondrous Will is done.

Lord make me quick to share a joke in passing
With laughing children or a nearby friend
To cheer the day away without complaining
Seeking a little happiness to spend.

England once had thousands of windmills with sails turning slowly and majestically. Only a few survive; the one opposite is at Pitstone, Bucks., the other is Hunsett Mill in Norfolk.

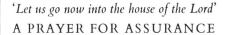

'Let us go now into the house of the Lord'
A PRAYER FOR ASSURANCE

It is Thy hand that I am clasping
And Thy guidance that I seek.
It is Thy love that I am asking
And Thy voice if Thou wilt speak.
It is Thy house I hope to enter
And Thy face I long to see
Guide me, guard me in thy Truth
For I am nothing without Thee.

Castle Combe, Wiltshire

Flower arranging can be a very satisfying hobby, especially if your own garden supplies the flowers you use.

'Be ye kind one to another'
PRAYER FOR PATIENCE

Lord make me kind to those I do not care for
The pompous people and prosaic bores.
Let me find time to say a quiet prayer for
The tiresome few who only talk of chores.

Help me to help the world and not to hinder
Nor lose my love towards my fellow folk,
Nor be indifferent to another's talent
With ridicule and the unkindly joke.

Nor yet to throw disdain upon new projects
Nor use my age to quench the fires of youth.
Lord make me kind when feeling most contrary
That gentleness may always ride with truth.

Take my deeds and make them better
Know my thoughts and make them kind
For I am full of frailties, Lord,
The way I was designed.

Guard me, guide me, love me
Unworthy though I be
That every hour of every day
I nearer grow to Thee.

Opposite: Canterbury has become a city where old and new
mix happily. This picture shows an old part of the city –
Butchery Lane. *Above:* in deepest Suffolk – Hitcham.

'He drew me out of many waters'
THE CALL

Call Thou me and I will answer
Point the way and I will go
Speak to me and I will hear Thee
Make a sign and I will know.

Proud to follow where Thou leadest
Ready at Thy least bequest.
Here I am to do Thy bidding
Offering my feeble best.

Coverack, Cornwall

'It is I – be not afraid'

THE LONELY NIGHT

Lonely is the night
When those we love are far away
For it is dark at eventide
'Lord Jesus light the way'.

Touch my life with sympathy
That all men's ways are known
That I may notice other troubles
And forget mine own.

Above: Aylesford is a famous beauty-spot on the River Medway in Kent. *Right:* the cathedral at Chichester in Sussex, founded *c.* 1091 by Bishop Ralph.

The day has reached the eventide
The time when shadows fall
And friends that we have loved and lost
Are missed the most of all.

Bring Thy comforts to our thinking
Blessed with memories we have known
Give us courage for our duties
And the faith to live alone.

It is possible to pay up to fifty guineas for a pedigree cat, yet most people find happiness in the nondescript variety as shown in these pictures.

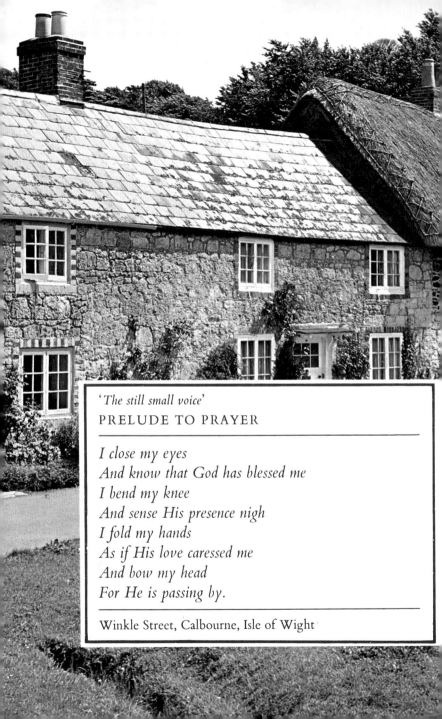

'*The still small voice*'
PRELUDE TO PRAYER

I close my eyes
And know that God has blessed me
I bend my knee
And sense His presence nigh
I fold my hands
As if His love caressed me
And bow my head
For He is passing by.

Winkle Street, Calbourne, Isle of Wight

'He leadeth me beside the still waters'
THE DAY IS ENDING

This life, though but a lovely day is ending
The sun has set above the highest hill.
I know not yet what way I may be wending
But I will close my book for good or ill.

There will be loving friends to wait my coming
To stretch a hand and draw me home to Thee
And kindly kin who have gone on before me
And loved ones I am longing now to see.

Give me Thy hand to cling to in the darkness
Give me Thy love to light the path ahead.
Give me Thy wisdom when my courage falters
Thy holy light to shine where I must tread.

Water has a subtle, calming influence on the mind of man and is often associated with scenes of great beauty. *Opposite:* Rydal Water in the Lake District was loved by Wordsworth. *Above:* in the Trossachs – Loch Achray, Perthshire.

MIRACLES

Glimpse a sunbeam on a petal
Catch the dew upon a leaf
Watch the shimmer of a butterfly
And dare to lack belief.

Touch a twig and see the tracery
Of growing grass about
Then dare to doubt a Greater Mind than man's
Has worked it out.

Butterflies – the most colourful of English insects. *Opposite:* a Red Admiral. *Above:* Tortoiseshell.

'Call upon me in the day of trouble'
IN BEREAVEMENT

Sad is my heart and great my loss
And lone the way I go
But loving Thee the more
It is the only way I know.

Comfort me Lord with the star of the evening
Comfort me Lord with the song of the sea
With hills and heather, with rain and roses
In the sparkle of water, O Lord comfort me.

Aysgarth Falls, Yorkshire

Above: ponies can be great fun for children – look at the envious looks that the two riders are getting from the others! The location is Hanmer, Flintshire. *Opposite:* a pause for a chat at Birdbrook, Essex.

May I remember as the years climb onwards
That I was young so short a time ago.
I, also filled the dwelling place with muddle
Singing as loudly as my voice would flow.

May I refrain from making caustic comments
And be content with tasks within my scope
Filling the longer leisure hours with interest
Never losing sight of faith and hope.

May I remember all the high excitement
Anger and laughter, boisterous and loud
That I may live with tolerance and kindness
Remembering when I was young and proud.

Don't expect a miracle to happen straight away
When in your extremity you found time to pray.
Have faith to go on praying, go on working too
Problems worry everyone on earth, not only you.

Leave your health in God's good keeping
And let your fears go free
Give Him time . . . and never say
'God has forgotten me'.

The glorious scenery of Scotland is at its best in Autumn when the foliage takes on its fiery hues. *Left:* Loch Tummel, Perthshire. *Above:* Loch Ewe from Inverewe Gardens, Ross.

'*Seekest thou good things for thyself? – seek them not!*'
PRAYERS FOR PEACE

*Politics and problems of the world are too
involved, too far off to envisage and too
savage to be solved by those of simple purpose
counting every man his brother. Seeing only
one way – being kind to one another.
Wilt Thou accept our prayers and make these
fearful terrors cease, and in Thy greater
wisdom bring forth tolerance with peace?*

Wintertime, Tal-y-llyn, Merioneth, Wales

'The night cometh when no man can work'

SO ENDS THE DAY

As the day goes out with the setting sun
Forgive the tasks that are left undone.
As the long night ends and the new day starts
Renew the zest in our weary hearts.

As hands grow listless and feet feel tired
Recall the wishes that were desired.
And lead us on over trial and sorrow
To another chance on a new tomorrow.

Here the sun sets with breathtaking beauty behind the quiet
village church of Wreningham in Norfolk.

85306 365 6 © *1972 Jarrold & Sons Ltd, Norwich*
Published and Printed in Great Britain by Jarrold & Sons Ltd, Norwich. 172